T0207763

THE PRACTICAL STRATEGIES SERIES
IN GIFTED EDUCATION

series editors

FRANCES A. KARNES & KRISTEN R. STEPHENS

A Menu of Options for Grouping Gifted Students

Karen B. Rogers

Routledge
Taylor & Francis Group

NEW YORK AND LONDON

First published 2006 by Prufrock Press Inc.

Published 2021 by Routledge
605 Third Avenue, New York, NY 10017
2 Park Square, Milton Park, Abingdon, Oxon OX14 4RN

*Routledge is an imprint of the Taylor & Francis Group,
an informa business*

© 2006 by Taylor & Francis

Notice:
Product or corporate names may be trademarks or registered
trademarks and are used only for identification and
explanation without intent to infringe.

ISBN 13: 978-1-59363-192-5 (pbk)

Contents

The Practical Strategies Series in Gifted Education offers teachers, counselors, administrators, parents, and other interested parties up-to-date instructional techniques and information on a variety of issues pertinent to the field of gifted education. Each guide addresses a focused topic and is written by scholars with authority on the issue. Several guides have been published. Among the titles are:

- *Acceleration Strategies for Teaching Gifted Learners*
- *Curriculum Compacting: An Easy Start to Differentiating for High-Potential Students*
- *Enrichment Opportunities for Gifted Learners*
- *Independent Study for Gifted Learners*
- *Motivating Gifted Students*
- *Questioning Strategies for Teaching the Gifted*
- *Social & Emotional Teaching Strategies*
- *Using Media & Technology With Gifted Learners*

For a current listing of available guides within the series, please contact Prufrock Press at (800) 998-2208 or visit http://www.prufrock.com.

In the past 15 years, the issues surrounding ability grouping have been thoroughly, and at times, heatedly, discussed and debated. In a recent, exhaustive search of the research, it was found that much of what we already knew about ability and performance grouping for gifted children has not changed. What has changed, however, is that a greater number of grouping types have been researched. Newer studies have looked more closely at effects other than achievement on students, so a better understanding regarding the social and emotional impact of certain forms of grouping on students is emerging. The purpose of this guide is to bring readers up-to-date on this research as it pertains to gifted learners, so they can have confidence when making decisions regarding grouping gifted learners.

This publication is composed of two distinct sections. The first identifies and defines the four forms of grouping gifted children by ability and the six forms of grouping based on performance. Research from the last 10 years is discussed for each of these grouping options. The second section of this guide focuses on how to choose the *right* form of grouping and how to implement it in a school setting, while considering administrative, teaching, and curricular factors. Two tables have been included to help understand the different roles a regular classroom teacher and a gifted resource teacher might play within each grouping option and to help implement curricula and instructional strategies most appropriate for each form of grouping. In addition, a list of select resources that might be helpful in setting up and implementing each grouping option has also been included.

In general, almost any form of grouping provides an academic or achievement gain to gifted learners with fairly positive social and emotional gains, as well. Grouping tends to be the "least restrictive environment" for gifted learners, and the most effective and efficient means for schools to provide more challenging coursework, giving these children access to advanced content and providing them with a peer group.

Grouping is a vehicle educators can use to allow gifted learners access to learning at the level and complexity necessary. It is probably more important to spend time thinking about what these learners will actually do once they are grouped, than what form of grouping is to be selected.

Can You Name the Grouping Options?

For each of the italicized options in the two case studies below, see if you can identify the grouping option. Space has been provided for your answers beneath each case study. The correct answers can be found at the end of this publication (see pp. 43–44).

Case Study 1: Susanna

Susanna was reading well before she entered kindergarten. Her kindergarten teacher sent her to the *first grade's top reading class* for reading instruction, where she held her own with her older peers. In first through third grade, Susanna was part of the *top reading group at each grade level*. In third grade, she was also invited to join the Challenge *resource room pull-out program* in which research skills, critical thinking, and creative productivity were taught to the brightest youngsters by a gifted and talented resource teacher. In grades four through six, Susanna was allowed to *move beyond grade level in both reading and mathematics*. She completed sixth grade work in fifth grade, and she worked on middle school materials *on her own* throughout fifth and sixth grade. In middle school, Susanna was provided with trimesters of *gifted seminar classes* in the humanities and was placed in the *accelerated mathematics classes*. She completed algebra I and II while still in middle school. In her first 2 years of high school, Susanna was placed in *accelerated mathematics classes* and in *honors English, social studies, and science classes*. Her junior year she took calculus within the *Advanced Placement (AP) program*. She also took *AP classes* in English, social studies, and science her final two years of high school. What were Susanna's grouping options?

1. First grade's top reading class in kindergarten

   _____

2. Top reading group at each grade level

   _____

3. Resource room pull-out program

   _____

4. Move beyond grade level in both reading and mathematics

   _____

5. On her own

   _____

6. Gifted seminar classes

   _____

7. Accelerated mathematics classes

   _____

8. Honors English, social studies, and science classes

   _____

9. Advanced Placement program

   _____

10. AP classes

   _____

Case Study 2: Antonio

Antonio was tested on his math and reading prowess, as well as his general aptitude for learning in kindergarten, and was then placed in a first grade heterogeneous *class that held the eight brightest children* at that grade level. His teacher would spend about one third of her instructional time differentiating math, reading, and social studies for this group of students. They would then work as *two small groups, cooperatively*, on assigned tasks, while the teacher worked with the remainder of the students each day. This placement continued for Antonio throughout his elementary school years. In third grade, Antonio was invited to join various *short-term enrichment experiences* in areas where he showed proficiency. His favorite experiences were with "Writer's Workshop" and "Experimental Science Design." In middle school, Antonio was placed in a *highly gifted program* in which the brightest children from across his school district were all housed in one middle school. The program contained *students from grades 6, 7, and 8,* and each student worked at the pace and level of complexity he or she was capable of with others who were at the same place in the curriculum, regardless of their grade or age. In high school, Antonio enrolled in the Pre-International Baccalaureate (Pre-IB) and *International Baccalaureate program* (IB), taking all the required courses necessary for completing his IB Diploma. In his senior year, he also attended a *class offered by the local college* on his high school campus before the official school day began. What were Antonio's grouping options?

1. Class that held the eight brightest children

    _____

2. Two small groups, cooperatively

    _____

3. Short-term enrichment experiences

    _____

4. Highly gifted program

_____

5. Students from grades 6, 7, and 8

_____

6. International Baccalaureate program

_____

7. Class offered by the local college

_____

Both Susanna and Antonio were given the advantage of grouping options based on their ability or aptitude levels, regardless of how well they were performing. Susanna enjoyed two of those options in her K–12 experience: the Challenge resource room pull-out program in her elementary years and the humanities seminar in her middle school years. Antonio was engaged in several of these ability-grouping options: cluster grouping and like-ability cooperative grouping in his elementary years, and the self-contained multiage class in his middle school years.

In general, there are four ability-grouping options for bright children, but many permutations of these four options can be derived from them, depending upon the setting in which they are offered. The four options are *full-time ability grouping, cluster grouping, pull-out enrichment groups,* and *like-ability cooperative groups*. Each of these will be defined and described and the research that supports or does not support the option will be discussed. Knowledge of the actual research on these options is important for both parents and teachers to utilize when they get ready to propose or put a grouping option into practice. Too often in schools, grouping practices have been tried without any regard to what previous research had to say about their effects, or lack thereof. Predictably, then, the practice is disbanded 2–3 years later and due to this, two to three grade levels of gifted children have lost the beneficial academic achievement gains they might have been able to make otherwise. If there were no research to support an option, then it would be important for educators to try a new practice and document its outcomes for learners, but when there is consistent and positive research, there is a strong likelihood that the practice will succeed and endure.

What have been particularly helpful for both parents and educators in the past 15 years are the many meta-analyses of research. Meta-analysis is the process of combining the results of related studies. Seventeen such compilations have been created about gifted learners. This makes it possible for readers to gauge the potential academic, social, and psychological effects and how strong those effects are, by taking into account every study that exists on the practice, just by studying the meta-analysis. The only caveat to this, however, is that the meta-analysis represents an average effect across all the studies; there may not be a single study among the group that describes the specific school setting of the educator or parent reading the meta-analysis. Study the long list of study references at the end of these publications, and scan the study titles, looking for relevant school settings (e.g., "in a rural elementary school" or "in a large urban setting in the Midwest"). If similar school settings are there, than the practice described will probably work well for the parent or educator reading the meta-analysis. If there are no relevant studies, then perhaps he or she will want to try the practice, but take care in monitoring that it is working similarly to what was described in the meta-analysis; in other words, documenting local results and the new practice's impact on gifted learners. It is likely there will be support nearby in the form of a local college or university, which can provide research students who can help with research design, data collection, and data analysis and interpretation.

Full-Time Ability Grouping

An IQ or aptitude test score typically identifies students selected for this option. Those students meeting or exceeding the set criterion level (e.g., 130 IQ), would be placed with similar ability students in the same, self-contained, homogeneous classroom for the majority of each school day, often year after year. The teacher of this self-contained classroom would then differentiate every subject area appropriately to meet the needs for the whole-to-part, fast-paced, complex, and conceptual learning known to be common in intellectually gifted learners. The teacher would take great care to eliminate excess drill and practice, understanding that this can actually damage the long-term encoding of knowledge and skills for these learners, especially in science and mathematics.

James and Chen-Lin Kulik have conducted at least five meta-analyses of all the research on full-time ability grouping in magnet schools, special schools for the gifted, or full-time self-contained gifted classrooms in a school-within-a-school situation. Their results, spanning the period from 1982 to the present, have been remarkably consistent. At the K–6 grade levels, gifted learners are likely to accomplish approximately 1½ years of curriculum in all subject areas for each year they are in such a program, when compared to equally gifted children placed in heterogeneous classrooms. In grades 7–12, gifted learners accomplish approximately 1⅓ years of curriculum in all subject areas per year. These comparative gains can be made even greater, according to Kulik (1993), when the curriculum itself is adjusted more fully. Effect sizes (ES), which is the estimate of expected achievement gain, ranged from .41 (1⅖ years' gain) for enriched classes, in which conceptual thinking, complexity, elimination of drill and practice, and whole-to-part organization of knowledge acquisition were practiced, to .87 (1⅘ years' gain) when the knowledge was greatly compacted and the pace of presentation was increased to two to three times the normal class pace (Kulik & Kulik, 1992).

The socialization and psychological outcomes of this form of grouping have also been studied extensively in recent years.

The Kuliks (1992) have conducted four meta-analyses of research on self-esteem effects, and have found that gifted children in mixed-ability classes have somewhat higher global self-esteem than do gifted children in full-time program placements. Many, including Gross (1997), have argued that children in full-time programs acquire more realistic perceptions of their self-esteem than those children in a mixed-ability class, who may have inflated perceptions because they are undoubtedly the "stars." Keller (1991) compared the cognitive, social, and global self-perceptions of gifted children in mixed-ability classes, continuous progress programs, and a gifted magnet school. It was found that cognitive self-perceptions were highest in the mixed-ability setting, followed by the continuous progress setting, but social self-perceptions were highest in the magnet school setting. There were no differences among the gifted in their global sense of worth within any of the three settings.

What happens when a gifted child is placed in a heterogeneous setting without others like him- or herself? Kennedy (2002) described a case study of a 9-year-old gifted boy in a fifth grade classroom of 29 students. She was able to document satisfactory achievement in his academics, but noted that he literally had no friends and used the teacher as his intellectual peer, demanding much of the teacher's one-on-one time.

Motivation for learning is another outcome affected by grouping or the lack of grouping. According to the Kuliks (1992), gifted learners show substantial gains in interest for the subjects studied when grouped with others of like-ability (ES = .27), but general motivation for learning and attitude toward school become only slightly more positive (ES = .11). In an interesting case study of one school restructured on Sizer's Coalition of Essential Schools (Sizer, 1984, 1992, 1996), in which all grouping and honors classes were eliminated, Lynch (1993) tracked a gifted 10th grade girl who continued to show motivation to learn in the first year of restructuring, but was dissatisfied with the level of difficulty of the work she was given. Lynch expressed concerns that if she did not personally make the effort to reach out for more challenges, she might be limiting her options.

Shields (2002) compared both achievement and self-perception outcomes of gifted and regular students in homogeneous and mixed-ability classes, finding that the achievement gains of the gifted were substantially greater in homogeneous settings, and that for regular and lower achieving students in homogeneous settings, there were no detrimental self-perceptions or attitudes toward school. In homogeneous settings, however, the gifted were more likely to work on the development of career interests while regular and low achievers in such settings showed greater academic self-confidence. The gifted in homogeneous settings reported that their teachers reinforced self-concept, had higher expectations, gave more feedback on their performance, gave more homework, and spent more classroom time on academic learning than was reported by gifted students in mixed-ability settings. In a comparison of four forms of programming arrangements, Delcourt, Loyd, Cornell, and Goldberg (1994) found that gifted students in special schools showed substantially more positive attitudes towards learning than did students in resource room pull-out programs, separate regrouped classes, or within-class regrouped classes.

In sum, the research on gifted students placed full-time with others of like-ability, whether this is a full-time program, a school-within-a-school, a special school for the gifted, or a self-contained class for gifted learners, clearly documents substantial academic gains and increases in motivation toward the subjects being studied. Their already more positive attitude toward learning is maintained in these settings, and their perceptions of challenge and social outlets are substantially improved. Gifted students' academic self-esteem is more realistic in this type of setting, not unrealistically high as can happen when they have only nongifted students with whom to compare their abilities.

Cluster Grouping

Cluster grouping is when five to eight students, identified for having the highest aptitude or IQ test scores at a given grade level, are placed together as a group in an otherwise heteroge-neous classroom with a teacher who: (1) wants to have them; (2) is trained to know how to differentiate for them; and (3) devotes a proportionate amount of classroom time to the differ-entiation of their curriculum and instruction. In most cases, the teacher will increase the presentation pace to two to three times the normal class pace, teach concepts whole-to-part, eliminate excess drill and practice, and compact what the small group already has mastered. Approximately one third of the teacher's instructional time would be spent working with this small group, while the remainder of the class worked on their assigned tasks. This group would then work independently or in small groups for two thirds of their classroom time, while the teacher worked with the remainder of the class.

The research on this option has shown even greater aca-demic gains for gifted learners than with full-time, self-con-tained classes, perhaps because a group of 5–8 students will be more homogeneous than a group of 24–30, allowing the pace and complexity to be kept high. In general, clustered gifted stu-dents make about $1\frac{3}{5}$ of a year's gain when compared to equally gifted children in a heterogeneous classroom without grouping of any kind (Kulik & Kulik, 1992). In Gentry's (1999) causal-comparative, longitudinal study of cluster grouping practices, she found the number of students identified as gifted increased for each year they were present in a cluster classroom. In other words, other students placed in a room with the cluster group seemed to benefit from the differentiated instruction, as well. In addition, Gentry reported statistically significant achieve-ment growth for the clustered gifted students, in part due to high teacher expectations, as well as the differentiation that could be documented.

In Schuler's (1997) report of a national survey on cluster grouping practices, it was found that of those who responded, 61 of the 69 districts (representing 15 states) made the cluster size one third of the class's composition. The practice was more likely to be used in grades 3–5, but 12% of the districts were using cluster grouping in grades 10–12. Observations made by these respondents suggested that the instruction in cluster classrooms was qualitatively different, with the teachers more likely to use content enrichment, thinking skills, and content differentiation in such settings. Feelings of educators in these districts were mixed, with approximately 13% of the administrators feeling negatively toward the option. Nevertheless, more than 90% of the districts reported very positive attitudes toward school and learning among the students who were placed in cluster classrooms. In further research, Gentry (1996) reported that low achieving and regular students seem to flourish when the brightest students have been removed from their classroom. For the clustered students, test score performance increased dramatically on the Iowa Tests of Basic Skills (ITBS) and the California Achievement Test (CAT) for each year they were in a cluster classroom.

In sum, the research suggests that gifted students placed in cluster classrooms experience substantial academic gains in achievement and have more positive attitudes toward learning and school than do gifted students in other settings. The level of differentiation in these classrooms is considerably different than what is found in other program arrangements. Regular students seem to benefit, as well. If they are in the cluster classroom, more of them perform better academically and if they are in a nonclustered classroom in the same school, they tend to perform at higher levels, becoming the new "stars" in the classrooms from which the gifted have been removed.

Pull-Out Grouping

When students identified by high test scores are removed from their regular classrooms for a specific period of time each week to work on general intellectual skills with a gifted resource teacher, the concept of an ability-grouped, resource room pull-out program is implemented. The levels of motivation and persistence, as well as the quality of performance may often differ among the children identified for this form of grouping, thereby making the teacher's job in differentiating all the more difficult. Because this option is often held from one hour to one day a week, it is also difficult for consistent follow-through among students. This is often a popular option among administrators because it does stand alone as a recognizable program, and among students because it varies from their regular education program.

In 1985, Cox, Daniel, and Boston found that more than 80% of the districts they surveyed used resource room pull-out programming as their only gifted option. Vaughn, Feldhusen, and Asher (1991) reported that resource room pull-out programs that focused on critical thinking skills over the course of a year resulted in gains equivalent to two fifths of a year additional gain and an additional one third of a year gain for creative thinking. Such gains were present only when the entire year's focus was on one form of skill development, rather than the usual "hodgepodge" of experiences offered in many resource room pull-out gifted programs. In an interesting interview survey study by Campbell and Verna (1998), in which the researchers compared resource room pull-out programs for the gifted (n = 18) and separate full-time classes for the gifted (n = 39), they found that administrators tended to monitor resource room pull-out programs more closely and to better provide differentiated materials and experiences for this type of program than for separate classes. Teachers in the separate classes also reported feeling a much heavier burden in having to constantly differentiate their curriculum for bright students.

Zeidner and Schleyer (1999) compared a variety of emotional variables among gifted students placed in a full-time setting or in a regular classroom with one day a week in a resource room pull-out program in Israeli schools (n = 763). They reported that the regular pull-out students exhibited greater anxiety, but had higher academic self-concepts and more positive perceptions of their giftedness than did gifted children in a special school. However, students in the special schools were more positive about school and their school environment, and showed more motivation for learning in their program of study.

In sum, the research suggests that there is substantial improvement in skill development, such as in critical or creative thinking when these are the focus of the resource room pull-out program. More differentiated materials are provided to teachers in pull-out programs than for those in other grouping options, thereby requiring less personal effort in differentiation than in other options. The self-concept of gifted learners is higher in resource room pull-out programs than in other gifted groupings and their perceptions of giftedness are also more positive, but there seems to be less motivation for learning and accepting challenges than in other grouping options.

Like-Ability Cooperative Grouping

Like-ability cooperative grouping occurs within a heterogeneous classroom of students, when a teacher groups three to four of the brightest (as identified by aptitude or IQ test scores) students together and assigns them a differentiated task or project that they work on cooperatively and are evaluated on jointly. Other groupings in the same classroom might also be like-ability or more mixed in composition. In the case of Antonio's cluster classroom, his teacher would have made two like-ability cooperative groups out of the eight children that comprised the gifted cluster. In most cases, the cooperative tasks assigned to these groups would span a longer time period, in addition to extending beyond regular curriculum standards and skills.

Research on this type of option has taken two forms in recent years. Until 1990, research suggested some socialization gains within these groups for children with disabilities, English language learners, and for achieving students, but claims for achievement gains were unsubstantiated (Roy, 1990). Since 1990, the research has focused more on the comparative benefits to gifted learners of mixed-ability versus like-ability cooperative learning groups. Arneson and Hoff (1992) reported that gifted students do not see cooperative learning as a primary venue for developing or maintaining relationships. The authors recommended that cooperative learning be used with gifted learners not as a primary source of either learning or socialization, but only as a supplementary experience.

Stout (1993) experimented with using cooperative learning with elementary gifted students in a resource room pull-out setting, finding that the gifted students demonstrated very good social and academic behaviors in their cooperative groups and that academic achievement was not lowered by this form of grouping, but the pace of group work was substantially slower than when these children worked either in whole group or individually in the resource room pull-out setting. Neber, Finsterwald, and Urban (2001) conducted a meta-analysis of 12 published studies on cooperative learning for gifted and high achieving students, finding that the studies conducted were generally methodologically unsound, restricted the spectrum of participants, used too simplistic materials to accurately measure achievement gains, and provided restricted outcomes. The researchers concluded that high-ability students learn better in homogeneous groups or individually than in cooperative settings. Kenny, Archambault, and Hallmark (1995) studied the effects of group composition on gifted and nongifted elementary students, concluding that there were no substantial differences in achievement for gifted learners whether mixed-ability or like-ability cooperatively grouped, nor any differences in self-concept or popularity. The mixed-ability groups, however, were hardest socially on nongifted students. Others in their cooperative triad, the average-ability student and the lower achieving student, did not want to work with each other again, and global self-perceptions declined somewhat.

In an 18-week intervention using cooperative learning and Gardner's multiple intelligence theory as the curriculum base, Martin, Powers, Ward, and Webb (2000) found that students were unable to transfer the skills they had learned beyond the actual tasks provided to the gifted and nongifted students in the cooperative learning settings. Although both groups of students generally preferred cooperative grouping, less time was spent on homework, and there were no changes in achievement levels. It should be noted that the regular classes ($n = 2$) were mixed-ability cooperative groups, while the two gifted classes were like-ability cooperative groups.

All of this research seems to fly in the face of Coleman, Gallagher, and Nelson's (1993a) survey of educator perceptions of the impact of cooperative learning. In their survey of 301 educators, who were either associated with gifted education or with the cooperative learning movement, there were significantly different views on the efficacy of cooperative learning. The educators associated with gifted education reported that the curriculum provided in cooperative learning settings was not challenging enough for gifted students, and often put these children in the role of a second teacher. The educators associated with cooperative learning felt that gifted students would acquire higher self-esteem and leadership skills by becoming team leaders in cooperative settings. Hernandez-Garduno (1997) also looked at cooperative grouping for statistics and probability, finding no differences in self-efficacy or achievement among those taught cooperatively and those taught in whole group, both competitively and individually. There were significantly more positive attitudes toward mathematics in the whole group method, as well as more voiced self-revelations about how answers were obtained and how problems were solved among the gifted in the whole group method.

In sum, the research on like-ability cooperative learning suggests possible achievement gains if and when the curriculum itself has been appropriately modified and differentiated. It does not seem to improve self-perceptions or socialization among the gifted, but it does not damage these aspects either. There is no support for mixed-ability cooperative learning providing any type of benefit for gifted learners.

Grouping by Performance Options

Both Susanna and Antonio experienced some performance grouping options as a part of their K–12 school experiences. In general, there are six such options:

1. regrouping for specific instruction,
2. cluster grouping,
3. within-class/flexible grouping,
4. like-performing cooperative learning,
5. cross-grade/multi-age grouping, and
6. resource room pull-out enrichment clusters.

Susanna was regrouped for reading in her early years in school and for other curricular areas in her high school years. Her Advanced Placement courses represented another form of regrouping, as well. She was also cross-graded in her earlier years. Antonio experienced enrichment clusters in his elementary years, multiage continuous progress in his middle school years, and substantial regrouping in his high school years, all based upon his performance in specific subjects, rather than his natural ability. Hence, the general difference between grouping by ability and grouping by performance is that group placement is based on observable performances in the latter, rather than on a child's potential, as in the former method. This would also suggest that differentiation in performance grouping is based on extending the child's knowledge and skills beyond the regular curriculum more than developing latent potential. This form of grouping option, because of its more intense focus on talent development, does not allow for the nurture or support of underachieving, at-risk, or undermotivated learners.

Regrouping for Specific Instruction

Regrouping for specific instruction is probably the most widely used form of performance grouping in settings that cater to gifted learners. In elementary school, this might be experienced as separate classrooms at each grade level where learners go depending on their curriculum level. Teacher A might be teaching those learners who are in the *Over the Rainbow* book in reading, while Teacher C teaches students who are in the *Under the Bridge* book. In middle school, pre-Advanced Placement or pre-International Baccalaureate programs might represent advanced-level classes, or there might be advanced, honors, general, and basic classes offered for each curricular area. In high school, International Baccalaureate or Advanced Placement courses are venues for higher performing students, as are honors or accelerated classes, college-level classes, and classes that require extensive prerequisites before students may enroll.

Slavin's (1987) research on this form of grouping provides substantial support for regrouping for specific instruction when students are appropriately matched to the level of curriculum being offered in the regrouped classes. Although students of all performance levels benefited from this form of regrouping, it was the high performing students who benefited most dramatically, making approximately $1\frac{1}{3}$ of a year gain in the area in which they were regrouped. The studies supporting this, however, demonstrate the actual curriculum in these classes had been substantially accelerated and made more complex. When curriculum was modified for regular and low achieving students, gains were also positive, but not so dramatic. Gamoran, Nystrand & Berends (1990) looked at eighth and ninth grade student achievement in English and history classes that had been regrouped, concluding that the high achieving regroupings resulted in greater academic gains, but that the decreases in achievement for the lower achieving regroups canceled out overall effects across the school. In other words, regrouping showed positive effects for higher achieving students, but did not show similar gains for those achieving at lesser levels. Their conclusion about canceling out effects seems rather simplistic and perhaps should be reconsidered. There probably is no "panacea" strategy for all levels of ability and performance; therefore, rejecting a strategy because it is not universal is neither viable nor logical.

James and Chen-Lin Kulik (1992) also found that motivation toward learning in a specific subject area was greatly improved, especially in science and social studies, when high performing students were regrouped and provided with differentiated curriculum and instruction. The Kuliks found, however, that general motivation for learning and for school was not substantially changed in regrouped settings.

Cluster Grouping

Just as with the small group of gifted children identified by a test score as possessing a particular aptitude or intelligence level and then placed in a heterogeneous class as a group for differentiated curriculum and instruction, this form of cluster grouping identifies children by their comparatively extraordinary performance rather than by their IQ score. For example, a cluster classroom holding the top eight mathematics students at a grade level is established. Alongside it a second cluster classroom of the top eight reading/language arts students is offered. These two cluster teachers will undoubtedly coordinate their differentiated teaching of reading and mathematics so that those students who are extraordinary in both subjects can partake in the higher differentiation offered by each cluster teacher. This might mean that both teach mathematics at the same time and then reading and language arts at the same time and the talented children from each cluster move accordingly to the higher or slightly lower level of differentiation they need in each subject.

At this time, there is little research on this form of cluster grouping, but the potential academic effects can be clearly assumed, when one looks at research for other grouping options, such as regrouping, and when appropriate differentiation is provided to a group of students at a specified level of curriculum mastery.

Within-Class/Flexible Grouping

In this form of performance grouping, each teacher divides his or her students into small groups according to how ready they are for the curriculum outcomes. For example, there might be a small group, the "red birds," who are having difficulty mastering longitude and latitude concepts, which are necessary for the upcoming map skills unit. This group will need remediation before actually beginning the unit. There might be a larger group of children in the classroom who are absolutely ready for the map skills unit, the "blue birds." And there may be a group of children, the "yellow birds," who have already mastered all the skills to be presented in the map unit. This group will need extensions beyond the unit if they are to continue to grow in their understanding of geography.

In recent years there has been some research supporting the within-class/flexible grouping option. Mousley (1998) interviewed teachers about their perceptions of their own role in teaching for mathematical understanding. He found that teachers tended to use within-class ability grouping to ease this understanding. They placed children in smaller groups by using curriculum-based tests from those units to be taught and then used the children's test performance as guides for instructional groupings and to guide the content and skills to be differentiated for the smaller groups. The groupings were not rigid, but rather formed based on the children's current level of mastery. Borton (1991) found that while teaching reading and mathematics in grades 3–4, having students regrouped within a classroom as gifted, regular, and bilingual led to more than one year's gain in those subjects for all three groups. Lou et al., (1996) compared all studies of within-class and whole class instruction and found that achievement was substantially greater for all performance level groups with within-class grouped instruction. When small heterogeneous groups were the comparison group, the homogeneously grouped children showed greater academic achievement, as well. Burnette (1999) found that within-class groups of 3–4 students were particularly effective in reading instruction, but only when the materials were appropriately differentiated. In terms of self-concept, Delcourt et al., (1994) found that gifted students in within-class groups tended to have higher academic self-concept than gifted students in special schools, special classes, or resource room pull-out programs.

Like-Performing Cooperative Grouping

Just as with like-ability cooperative grouping, each teacher places like-performing students together as a cooperative team and provides them with a differentiated task and set of expectations on which they will be evaluated. In a science unit on electricity, for example, the top four science students in the class work together in devising an electrical system out of a given set of materials while others in the class follow the prescribed science curriculum on electricity and systems.

Some research has been conducted on this form of grouping in the past few years. Elmore and Zenus (1994) found that highly gifted learners working together in an accelerated math curriculum learned more when learning cooperatively using the jigsaw method. In this method, individual students within each cooperative group take responsibility for a portion of the learning task and then share what they learn with the others in their group. They also found that lower achieving students benefited even more than the gifted when they were put together cooperatively with others at their own achievement level. Kanevsky (1985) compared gifted learners working in cooperative teams formed on performance level with gifted learners working competitively in computer-based mathematics instruction and found that these elementary students tended to prefer working in pairs competitively rather than cooperatively. In case studies of five schools that were successfully meeting the needs of gifted students, Coleman, Gallagher, and Nelson (1993b) discovered that these schools tended to allow the highly able students to work together cooperatively, finding that they tended to complain less about a lack of challenge, feelings of exploitation, and feelings of isolation. Brush (1997) studied the use of cooperative pairs working on Independent Learning Systems' mathematics activities, a curriculum that allows students to progress through a set curriculum at their own pace. A pair was comprised of one high performing student and one low achieving student or two like-performing students working cooperatively. He found that low achieving students, paired with high performers stayed on task significantly longer than when paired with another low achieving student. Likewise, two high performing students cooperatively teamed engaged in study for a longer time than two low achievers teamed, but no academic differences in achievement were found for either cooperatively grouped team.

Carter, Jones, and Rua (2001) also looked at the effects of dyad cooperative pairs in science education among fifth grade students in a suburban school. In this case, they compared high performing dyads with high-low performing dyads and concluded that gifted achievement in science is not dependent on whom the dyad partner is when the test covers traditional science materials. Carter and Jones have conducted several studies along this line throughout the 1990s and have never found achievement gains for higher performing students in these dyads. The gains have always been for the lower achiever of the dyad in nonacademic areas (i.e., less acting out, more acting like a student, etc.). The researchers claim their findings indicate that gifted learners do not construct knowledge differently than other learners, but more research needs to be done to ascertain the validity of this conclusion. If students are being measured with traditional materials and are cohering to a dyad mode of

cooperative learning, there is probably very little chance to determine how high performing learners construct knowledge on their own. Hollingsworth and Harrison (1999) compared whole class reading instruction with companion reading, a program that pairs a reader and nonreader to work cooperatively on reading fluency and comprehension. First grade students were placed in dyads, one high performing and one low performing, to use the materials of this reading program. In general, the researchers found that the dyads resulted in greater reading achievement than did whole group reading instruction, especially for the lower performing and at-risk students, but the highest performing readers in the dyads also achieved at higher levels than when they were instructed in the whole group method.

Cross-Graded/Multiage Classrooms

In cross-graded/multiage performance groupings, students are placed in classrooms either designated as a higher grade level (cross-graded) or without a grade level designation (multigrade) and are allowed to work at the level at which they are currently functioning. For the first form of this option, a fourth grader could be sent to sixth grade during math period or, if on a lower achievement level, could be sent to second grade during the math period. In order for this form of instruction to work, the school must follow a specified schedule for the teaching of mathematics each day. All grade levels would need to teach math at the same time so that children could freely participate in the appropriate level of math. In the multiage form of this strategy, each child would work on the materials at the level on which he or she is currently functioning, moving at an individual pace but working with whatever small group of students may be at the same place in the curriculum.

Since 1987, the research on cross-grade/multiage options has been positive, not only for gifted learners, but for all learners regardless of achievement level. Slavin (1987) reported an effect size of .45 (or about 1⅔ of a year gain) for elementary students of all abilities in reading when they were moved for reading instruction into the classroom that worked with their respective level of curriculum mastery. For example, a fourth grader needing to learn the skills of the second grade curriculum would work in the classroom focused on that level, and a fourth grader needing to learn skills beyond the fourth grade curriculum would work in the classroom at the more advanced level. He also reported an effect size of .46 for mathematics cross-grading. Rogers (1991) found that gifted students in nongraded/multiage classrooms had an effect size of .38 (approximately 1⅗ of a year gain) in all academic areas when allowed to move at the pace at which they were capable. Lloyd (1999) argued that teachers in multiage classrooms tend to be more likely to see the differences of high-ability children and to accommodate them. He also reported that gifted learners achieve at higher academic levels in these classrooms and there is a small, positive effect on their social and emotional development.

Hafenstein, Jordan, and Tucker (1993) studied the effects of gifted learners in a special school for the gifted, who were also multiage grouped, finding that most students, except for the oldest ones in the classroom, have generally positive perceptions of the arrangement. Teachers in these classrooms reported academic and leadership growth for the participating children. Burns and Mason (2002) studied 200 elementary schools with multiage classrooms and found that more high ability/high achieving students and students with high levels of independence were assigned to these classrooms and that when separate classrooms for the gifted were in place, these same students tended to be assigned to those classrooms. Simultaneously, there were significantly fewer low achieving/low independent students assigned to these classes. This would suggest that when such classes are chosen in a school, careful consideration is given to the kinds of students who will thrive in such a setting.

Performance-Based Send-Out Enrichment Clusters

When children with identifiable talents are selected to participate in a shorter-term resource room pull-out program to develop talent in that specified area, the ideal, performance-based pull-out program has been implemented. This would mean, for example, that the top creative writers at a grade level would come to work with an author for a 6-week writer's workshop that would develop and extend their creative writing skills, or that the top science students at a given grade level would work with a scientist from the university over a period of time to learn how to design experiments to answer their questions about a scientific phenomenon.

Although many descriptions of this type of program have been published in the last 10 years, few have systematically collected data on the academic effects of such an option. Vaughn et al., (1990) conducted a meta-analysis of existing studies, arguing that when the focus of the resource room pull-out program is a direct extension of an academic area integral to the school curriculum, the academic gains can be sizable. Lim (1994) reported that gifted students in Singapore, grades 7–10, reflected on positive self-esteem and self-concept development that occurred from participation in a resource room pull-out program in their journals, but that these students saw no real connection to schooling in such programs, even when these programs were designed to extend the regular curriculum.

Selecting and Implementing the Best Forms of Grouping for a School

From the review of recent research in the preceding sections of this guide, it is clear that schools have many choices, all of which will produce strong academic gains for gifted children when they are consciously grouped together for specified differentiation purposes. How does a school, then, decide which form of grouping is the best? There are three aspects that help with this decision:

1. administration factors,
2. teacher factors, and
3. curricular factors.

Administration Factors

The attitudes of school administration go far in making or breaking a program option. From the research reported here, it is clear that some factors tend to be more popular with administrators than others. A separate, recognizable gifted program, as often represented by the resource room pull-out program, is one option an administrator can tout to the public. Thus, it is often popular with administrators. A more integrated program, such as cluster classes, is more difficult to explain, even though it might offer gifted children daily differentiation in all academic areas that is consistent and well articulated. It is clear that administrators need to study the advantages and disadvantages of each form of grouping to help allay their concerns about how the public will perceive one option or another. In this era of data-driven, results-oriented decision making, there is a chance that administrators will opt for those research-supported options that provide the greatest academic gains, more so than in earlier times. But, whatever option is selected, additional personnel, materials, general upheaval to the schedule, personnel assignment, and explanations to the public must be considered if it is to succeed with the administrator. In this era of No Child Left Behind mandates, it has also become much more important to connect the outcomes expected academically from an option with the school's benchmarks for student achievement. Administrators do not want to neglect the needs of gifted children, but it must be clear that the options suggested would not require substantial effort that might detract from the academic goals of the rest of the school. Table 1 (see pp. 34–35) identifies the potential effort required to make each of the previously described grouping options work in a school setting.

A second administration factor relates to selecting options that mesh well with the size of the school population. Although cluster grouping may sound like a good idea, if the school is very small with only two classrooms per grade level and with only three children who would qualify for a cluster classroom, this might not be the option most favorable, nor would a special self-contained classroom be feasible, economically. For smaller schools, options such as within-class groupings, resource room pull-out programs that are cross-graded, or cross-grade grouping might be better options.

A third consideration among administration factors has to do with the identification process itself. The first step a school must undertake when selecting instructional management options, such as grouping, is to determine what kinds of gifts or talents are most evidenced in the school. Are there many high potential but underachieving students in the mix—children, for example, who have not had access to enrichments outside of school or whose families struggle for economic survival? If so, procedures must be used to identify potential rather than performance and options that involve grouping by natural ability rather than performance should be selected. But, if there seems to be a large group of high performing math students in the school or a large cluster of advanced readers, then performance grouping options should be considered. Identifying for natural ability or potential is most effective with the use of individually administered intelligence or aptitude tests, such as the Stanford-Binet V, the Wechsler Intelligence Scale for Children-IV (WISC-IV), the Woodcock-Johnson Assessment Scales, or the Kaufmann Assessment Battery for Children (K-ABC). These possess high enough ceilings and are less dependent on reading and writing skills in order to perform well. Group-administered paper-and-pencil tests are more problematic in locating high potential, at-risk learners.

There are several ways in which administrators can identify for high performance: (1) locally developed placement tests based on the school or district's curriculum standards; (2) custom-developed standardized tests, such as the Northwest Educational Assessment (NWEA), or (3) nationally normed standardized tests of achievement, such as the California Achievement Test (CAT), Iowa Tests of Basic Skills (ITBS), or the Stanford Achievement Test batteries, particularly if these latter instruments are administered above grade level (e.g., fifth grade form given to third grade high performers, etc.). The latter two options may require less work and expense than the use of locally developed tests, and also allow for performance beyond expected grade level. National standardized tests, for example, now have extensive norms for children considerably younger than the grade level at which the test is typically offered.

Teacher Factors

How teachers feel about certain options also plays a major role in how successfully a grouping option will be implemented in a school. As Table 1 emphasizes, each teacher in a school

Table 1
Requirements for Implementation
of Grouping Options in a School

Gifted Service	Regular Teacher Role	Gifted Resource Teacher Role
Full-Time Ability Grouping—Students are placed in a special school, a school-within-a-school, full-time gifted program, or magnet school based on their comparative ability.	Regular teachers have been extensively trained to know how to differentiate instruction and curriculum for gifted learners and have been transferred to this locale from other positions within the district.	Provides staff development to these regular teachers, provides differentiated materials or helps teachers adapt materials, works collaboratively in providing direct instruction in areas such as critical thinking, creative productivity, etc.
Cluster Grouping—Top 5–8 academically gifted students are placed with one teacher at a grade level and proportionate amount of that teacher's class time is spent in direct differentiation for this group. Remainder of class is normal mix of ability levels. Or, the top 5–8 math students are placed in one classroom and a concomitant reading/language arts cluster classroom is provided at each grade level.	One teacher at each grade level must be trained extensively in how to differentiate for the gifted and must be willing to take on this group. All academic areas will be differentiated for this cluster group on a daily basis.	Provides cluster teachers with enrichment materials, replacement units, collaborative teaching upon demand.
Critical Skills/Creative Skills or Academic Extension Pull-Out—Gifted students at a grade level are sent out for focused training in critical skills or creative skills or extensions of regular subject. Focus would be in one area only.	Compact regular curriculum so that gifted students will be free to be "pulled-out."	Implement pull-out focus as articulated curriculum from year to year. Design the enriched experiences included within the focus.
Like-Ability or Like-Performance Cooperative Groups—Each teacher groups brightest or highest performing students in classroom together to work on differentiated cooperative tasks.	Teacher preassesses mastery of regular curriculum outcomes and provides differentiated replacement tasks to the like-ability or like-performing group of students.	Provides teachers with preassessments, replacement cooperative tasks, direct instruction, supervision, or collaboration upon request.

Table 1
Requirements for Implementation
of Grouping Options in a School, continued

Gifted Service	Regular Teacher Role	Gifted Resource Teacher Role
Regrouping for Specific Instruction—All students at a grade level are regrouped by their achievement levels in a specific subject, such as reading or math. Curriculum in regrouped classrooms is appropriately differentiated for specific achievement level group.	Each teacher at a grade level is responsible for one achievement level classroom in the specific subject and will differentiate for that group.	Provides enrichment materials, units, collaborative teaching upon demand.
Within-Class Grouping—Each teacher sorts students according to their "readiness" for the upcoming curriculum to be implemented. Then differentiated curriculum and instruction are provided for each smaller group.	Teacher preassesses mastery of curriculum outcomes and provides differentiated tasks to smaller groups according to their readiness needs.	Provides preassessments, replacement units, direct instruction, supervision, or collaboration upon request.
Cross-Grade Grouping—All grade levels teach a specific subject at the same time of day so that all students can participate at the level in the curriculum where they are currently functioning, regardless of age or actual designated grade level.	Each teacher teaches the assigned grade level curriculum outcomes congruently to the students assigned to that classroom. In most cases, the teacher will not be teaching his or her actual grade level materials but will be assigned to another grade level to avoid issues with children who must attend "lower" level classes.	Provide extensions of each grade level's materials; help with preassessment and placement of children in correct readiness levels of the curriculum across all grades, upon request.
Multiage Classroom—Classrooms encompass three or more grades within each classroom so that students can work in a continuous progress mode, accomplishing the amount of curriculum they are capable of when they are ready to do so.	Each teacher preassesses where students should start in the curriculum and monitors their continuous progress from that point.	Provide extensions of each grade level's curriculum outcomes; help with preassessments and placement of children in correct readiness levels of the curriculum, upon request.

plays a role in every grouping option. In some cases, that role is primary and in others it is secondary, but the noncompliance of even one or a few teachers at a grade level or across grade levels destroys the needed articulation and congruence—hence, ultimate success—of an option. This would suggest that teachers need to give input on their preferences for a specific grouping option, which also assumes they have been given extensive information on what the research supports and what their roles would be for each grouping option considered.

Teachers' previous background and experiences with giftedness and talent plays a major role in the success of a grouping option's implementation, as well. If the school has had a resource room pull-out program for years and teachers saw this model as the "gifted program" and thereby were relieved of the responsibility of differentiating for their brightest students, elimination of the resource room pull-out option in lieu of mainstream differentiation may cause problems in which teachers balk at their increased workload and responsibility. If teachers' experiences with bright students have been primarily negative, they may be less willing to consider catering to the gifted in any form. If they have not had any experience with gifted learners, they may not see the need for differentiation at all. In effect, as grouping options are decided upon, it is critical that extensive staff development be in place before actual decisions for implementation or change are made in a school. Teachers will need to be apprised of what their personal responsibilities would be for each option being considered. At a minimum, Table 1 would be helpful information in the decision-making process.

Curricular Factors

In selecting a grouping option, in most cases, the "what" that will be taught is infinitely more important than how the children will be grouped or organized. Has money been set aside for the development or adaptation of differentiated curricular materials and staff development for teachers? Without the materials, it is likely that teachers will resort to "more of the same," providing busy work for gifted learners in their respective group rather than appropriately differentiated learning experiences. Table 2 suggests the types of curricula and curricular experiences highly able (gifted) and high performing (talented) students need in each grouping option. An inventory of what the school can provide along these lines might aid in the selection of the best grouping option. The good news is that there is sound and appropriate curricula already available. Some sources to consider include curricula by the College of William and Mary in science, social studies, and language arts for grades 2–10; and materials developed by Free Spirit Press, Great Potential Press, Prufrock Press, and Trillium.

A point of importance in the selection of a grouping option is the necessity of providing gifted students with the opportunity to be unique and to learn to work independently, as well. Finding the right mixture of like-ability/performance socialization and learning and individualized learning is difficult, but attainable. As noted in Table 2, in some instances individual projects and independent study can be incorporated within a grouping option quite fluidly and effectively.

Likewise, no matter which grouping option a school selects, it is important to assess the effectiveness of the decision through regular, annual assessment of student achievement gains and attitudes toward learning and school. If the expected effect sizes are not being registered, it will be important to reexamine the implementation of the option and reassess the quality of the curriculum being used and the differentiated delivery of that curriculum. Have the administration and the staff truly "bought" into the option selected? Why or why not? Have students indicated excitement over the experiences they are receiving? Are parents and the community supportive of the option being implemented? If yes is the answer to all these questions, then the signal is "go" for the succeeding year!

Table 2
Curricula Appropriate
for Each Grouping Option

Grouping Option	Content/Knowledge to Be Acquired	Skills to Be Developed
Full-Time Ability Grouping	Accelerated presentation pace in math and science; Open-ended problems; Study of people; Methods of inquiry; Discipline-based arts training—history, aesthetics; Service learning; Social issues discussions; Teaching games for review; Tutoring for remediation; Small group projects; Independent study projects; One-on-one tutoring; Literary "classics"; World's "great ideas" in philosophy, mathematics, science, and humanities; History; Regular challenge in all academic areas; Interdisciplinary curriculum units; Conceptual discussions; Dilemmas; Whole-to-part organization of content, concepts	Discovery learning; Higher order thinking; Inquiry learning; Creative problem-solving process; Critical thinking skills; Creative production skills; Communication skills; Self-direction skills; Self-awareness, self-concept skills; Socialization skills; Organization/time management skills; Problem-solving skills; Personal goal setting; Intuitive expression; Memory development; Proof and reasoning; Transformative products; Conflict resolution techniques
Cluster Grouping by Ability	Subject extension in all academic core areas; Accelerated presentation pace in math and science; Open-ended problems; Study of people; Methods of inquiry; Discipline-based arts training—history, aesthetics; Service learning; Social issues discussions; Teaching games for review; Small group projects; Literary "classics"; World's "great ideas" in philosophy, mathematics, science, and humanities; History; Regular challenge in all academic areas; Interdisciplinary curriculum units; Conceptual discussions; Dilemmas; Whole-to-part organization of content, concepts	Discovery learning; Higher order thinking; Inquiry learning; Creative problem-solving process; Critical thinking skills; Creative production skills; Communication skills; Self-direction skills; Self-awareness, self-concept skills; Socialization skills; Organization/time management skills; Problem-solving skills; Personal goal setting; Intuitive expression; Memory development; Proof and reasoning; Transformative products; Conflict resolution techniques
Pull-Out Grouped by Ability	Open-ended problems; Study of people; Methods of inquiry; Discipline-based arts training—history, aesthetics; Service learning; Social issues discussions; Small group projects; Independent study projects; Literary "classics"; World's "great ideas" in philosophy, mathematics, science, and humanities; History; Interdisciplinary curriculum units; Conceptual discussions; Dilemmas	Discovery learning; Higher order thinking; Inquiry learning; Creative problem-solving process; Critical thinking skills; Creative production skills; Communication skills; Self-direction skills; Self-awareness, self-concept skills; Socialization skills; Organization/time management skills; Problem-solving skills; Personal goal setting; Intuitive expression; Memory development; Proof and reasoning; Transformative products; Conflict resolution techniques
Like-Ability Cooperative Grouping	Extension of regular curriculum; Open-ended problems; Study of people; Methods of inquiry; Service learning; Social issues discussions; Small group projects; Literary "classics" literature circles; History; Interdisciplinary curriculum units; Conceptual discussions; Dilemmas	Discovery learning; Higher order thinking; Inquiry learning; Creative problem-solving process; Critical thinking skills; Creative production skills; Communication skills; Self-direction skills; Organization; time management skills; Problem-solving skills; Intuitive expression; Memory development; Proof and reasoning; Transformative products; Conflict resolution techniques
Regrouping by Performance Level for Specific Instruction	Accelerated presentation pace in math and science; Early content mastery; Subject acceleration; Whole-to-part organization of content, concepts;	Problem-based learning; Systematic feedback and its uses; Planning techniques; Personal goal setting; Memory development; Transformative products;

Table 2
Curricula Appropriate
for Each Grouping Option, continued

	Content/Knowledge to Be Acquired	Skills to Be Developed
Regrouping by Performance Level for Specific Instruction, continued	Teaching games for learning new information; Compacting; Individual projects; Independent study; Learning contracts; Tutoring for remediation; Lecture—concentrated information provision; Flexible task requirements, deadlines; Self-instruction materials; Consistent, daily challenge in talent area(s); Regular challenge in other academic areas; Talent development; Talent exhibition/competition	Real audiences for product evaluation; Individual benchmark setting
Cluster Grouping by Performance	Telescoping of learning time in talent area(s); Early content mastery; Subject acceleration; Teaching games for learning new information; Compacting; Individual projects; Independent study; Learning contracts; Lecture—concentrated information provision; Flexible task requirements, deadlines; Self-instructional materials; Consistent, daily challenge in talent area(s); Regular challenge in other academic areas; Talent development; Talent exhibition/competition	Discovery learning; Inquiry learning; Creative problem-solving process; Critical thinking skills; Creative production skills; Communication skills; Self-direction skills; Self-awareness, self-concept skills; Socialization skills; Organization/time management skills; Problem-solving skills; Intuitive expression; Memory development; Proof and reasoning; Transformative products
Within-Class Grouping	Telescoping of learning time in talent area(s); Early content mastery; Subject acceleration; Teaching games for learning new information; Compacting; Learning contracts; Flexible task requirements, deadlines; Self-instructional materials; Consistent, daily challenge in talent area(s)	Discovery learning; Inquiry learning; Creative problem-solving process; Critical thinking skills; Creative production skills; Communication skills; Self-direction skills; Self-awareness, self-concept skills; Socialization skills; Organization/time management skills; Problem-solving skills; Intuitive expression; Memory development; Proof and reasoning; Transformative products
Like-Performing Cooperative Groups	Telescoping of learning time in talent area(s); Early content mastery; Subject acceleration; Teaching games for learning new information; Compacting; Learning contracts; Flexible task requirements; deadlines; Self-instructional materials; Consistent, daily challenge in talent area(s)	Discovery learning; Inquiry learning; Creative problem-solving process; Communication skills; Self-direction skills; Socialization skills; Organization/time management skills; Problem-solving skills; Transformative products; Conflict resolution techniques
Cross-Grade/ Multiage Grouping	Early content mastery; Subject acceleration; Consistent, daily challenge in talent area(s); Telescoping of learning time in talent area(s); Learning contracts; Self-instructional materials	Discovery learning; Inquiry learning; Communication skills; Self-direction skills; Self-awareness, self-concept skills; Socialization skills; Organization/time management skills; Problem-solving skills; Intuitive expression; Proof and reasoning; Transformative products; Conflict resolution techniques
Pull-Out Enrichment Clusters	Telescoping of learning time in talent area(s); Early content mastery; Subject acceleration; Teaching games for learning new information; Lecture—concentrated information provision; One-on-one tutoring in talent area(s); Focused challenge in talent area(s); Real audiences for products; Talent development; Talent exhibition/competition	Discovery learning; Inquiry learning; Creative production skills; Communication skills; Self-direction skills; Self-awareness, self-concept skills; Socialization skills; Organization/time management skills; Problem-solving skills; Intuitive expression; Transformative products

Last Words and Next Steps

Few words have been spent on how the educator or parent goes about making the right match of gifted service to the documented abilities and talents of an individual child. That would be the subject of another publication. In fact, several books and articles have been written on just this set of strategies in the last few years. A few of these have been listed in the resource section of this publication. Informative Web sites that have dealt specifically with the grouping options and issues addressed in this publication have also been listed. This list of resources is the best way to bolster parents and teachers' educations in the research-based strategies for grouping gifted children.

Answers to Case Study One—Susanna:

1. First grade's top reading class in kindergarten
   Regrouping for specific subject
2. Top reading group at each grade level
   Regrouping for specific subject
3. Resource room pull-out program
   Pull-out enrichment groups
4. Move beyond grade level in both reading and mathematics
   Cross-grade grouping
5. On her own
   No grouping option
6. Gifted seminar classes
   Pull-out enrichment groups
7. Accelerated mathematics classes
   Regrouping for specific subject
8. Honors English, social studies, and science classes
   Regrouping for specific subject
9. Advanced Placement program
   Advanced Placement regrouping
10. AP classes
    Advanced Placement regrouping

Answers to Case Study Two—Antonio

1. Class that held the eight brightest children
   Cluster grouped classroom
2. Two small groups, cooperatively
   Like-ability cooperative grouping
3. Short-term enrichment experiences
   Enrichment clusters/send-out
4. Highly gifted program
   Special class/multiage classroom
5. Students in grades 6, 7, and 8
   Multiage/continuous progress
6. International Baccalaureate program
   International Baccalaureate regroup
7. Class offered by the local college
   College-in-the-schools regroup

Further Reading and Web Site Resources

Books and Monographs

Assouline, S., & Lupkowski-Shoplik, A. (2005). *Developing math talent: A guide for challenging and educating gifted students.* Waco, TX: Prufrock Press.

A guide to teaching mathematics to gifted students.

Brody, L. E. (Ed.). (2004). Grouping and acceleration practices in gifted education. In S. M. Reis (Series Ed.), *Essential readings in gifted education.* Thousand Oaks, CA: Corwin Press.

This is one in a collection of articles on grouping and acceleration pulled from previous *Gifted Child Quarterly* journals from the past 25 years.

Colangelo, N., & Davis, G. A. (2003). *Handbook of gifted education* (3rd ed.). Boston: Allyn and Bacon

This is a comprehensive text on the hot topics in gifted education written by experts in the field.

Corwin, M. (2000). *And still we rise: The trials and triumphs of twelve gifted inner-city high school students.* New York: William Morrow.

A reporter describes tribulations of Advanced Placement teachers in an inner city Los Angeles high school.

Kenny, D. A., Archambault, F. X., Jr., & Hallmark, B. W. (1995). *The effects of group composition on gifted and non-gifted elementary students in cooperative learning groups* (Research monograph). Storrs, CT: University of Connecticut.

This monograph gives a comparison of like-ability and mixed-ability cooperative learning in science.

Kulik, J. A. (1992). *An analysis of the research on ability grouping: Historical and contemporary perspectives.* Storrs, CT: The National Research Center on the Gifted and Talented.

This scholarly argument discusses the role ability grouping actually plays in the ultimate achievement of gifted learners.

Loveless, T. (1998). *The tracking and ability grouping debate.* Dayton, OH: Fordham Foundation.

This book provides a balanced review of research on full-time and part-time ability grouping across all ability groups.

Mathews, D. J., & Foster, J. F. (2005). *Being smart about gifted children: A guidebook for parents and educators.* Scottsdale, AZ: Great Potential Press.

A book of practical strategies for addressing major questions and debates about giftedness and its origins, including best practices to meet children's needs.

Olenchak, R. O. (1998). *They say my kid's gifted, now what? Ideas for parents for understanding and working with schools.* Waco, TX: Prufrock Press.

Easy-to-use guide for parents in selecting appropriate teachers and gifted programs for their children.

Rogers, K. (1991). *The relationship of grouping practices to the education of the gifted and talented learner: An executive summary.* Storrs, CT: The National Research Center on the Gifted and Talented.

This metaevaluation covers 13 meta-analyses of research on different forms of ability and performance grouping.

Rogers, K. B. (2002). *Re-forming gifted education: Matching the program to the child.* Scottsdale, AZ: Great Potential Press.

This book contains a comprehensive description of research on grouping, acceleration, and individualization practices used with gifted children.

Smutny, J. F. (2000). *Stand up for your gifted child: How to make the most of kids' strengths at school and at home.* Minneapolis, MN: Free Spirit Publishing.

Parents' guide to advocating for school options that differentiate the gifted child's academic learning.

Tallent-Runnels, M., & Candler-Lotven, A. C. (1996). *Academic competitions for gifted students: A resource book for teachers and parents.* Thousand Oaks, CA: Corwin Press.

Listing and contact information on several hundred group and individual competitions and contests gifted children can engage in both inside and outside of school.

Van Tassel-Baska, J., Benbow, C. P., & Feldhusen, J. F. (1998). *Excellence in educating gifted and talented learners* (3rd ed.). Denver: Love Publishing.

Comprehensive text on such subjects as grouping, acceleration, program development, and curriculum requirements of academic curricular areas.

Winebrenner, S. (2001). *Teaching gifted kids in the regular classroom: Strategies and techniques every teacher can use to meet the academic needs of the gifted and talented.* Minneapolis: Free Spirit Publishing.

Guide for teachers on how to cluster group and differentiate for gifted learners in a heterogeneous classroom setting.

Zaccaro, E. (2000). *Challenge math for the elementary and middle school student.* Bellevue, IA: Hickory Grove Press.

This book gives specific strategies and resources for teaching mathematics to gifted students.

Journal Articles

Hallinan, M. T., & Sorenson, A. B. (1985). Ability grouping and student friendships. *American Educational Research Journal, 22*, 485–499.

Large-scale study showing that children grouped with others of like-ability tend to select their friends from within that learning group.

Hoover, S. M., Sayler, M., & Feldhusen, J. F. (1993). Cluster grouping and elementary students at the elementary level. *Roeper Review, 16*, 13–15.

Survey of 46 Indiana school districts showing significant academic gains for cluster grouped gifted learners.

Web Sites

Hoagies' Gifted Education Page
http://www.hoagiesgifted.org

Lists numerous online and print resources for parents, educators, and gifted children.

Austega's Gifted Resource Centre
http://www.austega.com/gifted

Resources for parents and teachers of gifted children, developed in New South Wales, Australia.

ERIC Clearinghouse
http://www.ericec.org

Information on federally funded centers and sites.

National Association for Gifted Children
http://www.nagc.org

Resources, research, and general information on gifted children compiled by the largest gifted education organization in the United States.

References

Arneson, P., & Hoff, N. (1992). *Cooperative learning for the gifted student: Contributions from speech communication.* Paper presented at the annual meeting of the Speech Communication Association, Chicago. (ERIC Document Reproduction Service No. ED 353620)

Borton, W. M. (1991). *Empowering teachers and students in a restructuring school: A teacher efficacy interaction model and the effect on reading outcomes.* Paper presented at the annual meeting of the American Educational Research Association, Atlanta, GA. (ERIC Document Reproduction Service No. ED 335341)

Brush, T. A. (1997). The effects of group composition on achievement and time. *Journal of Research on Computing in Education, 30,* 2–18.

Burnette, J. (1999). Student groupings for reading instruction. *ERIC/OSEP Digest, E579.* (ERIC Document Reproduction Service No. ED 434435)

Burns, R. B., & Mason, D. A. (2002). Class composition and student achievement in elementary schools. *American Educational Research Journal, 39,* 207–233.

Campbell, J. R., & Verna, M. A. (1998). *Comparing separate class and pull-out programs for the gifted.* Paper presented at the annual meeting of the American Educational Research Association, San Diego, CA. (ERIC Document Reproduction Service No. ED 420953)

Carter, G., Jones, M. G., & Rua, M. (2001). Effects of partner's ability on the achievement and conceptual organization of high-achieving fifth-grade students. *Science Education, 87,* 94–111.

Coleman, M. R., Gallagher, J. J., & Nelson, S. (1993a). *Cooperative learning and gifted students: A national survey* (Research report for OERI). Washington, DC: Office of Educational Research and Improvement. (ERIC Document Reproduction Service No. ED 359717)

Coleman, M. R., Gallagher, J. J., & Nelson, S. M. (1993b). *Cooperative learning and gifted students: Report on five case studies* (Research report for OERI.) Washington, DC: OERI. (ERIC Document Reproduction Service No. ED 365008)

Cox, J., Daniel, N., & Boston, B. (1985). *Educating able learners: Programs and promising practices* (Report for the Richardson Foundation). Austin, TX: University of Texas.

Delcourt, M. A., Loyd, B. H., Cornell, D. G., & Goldberg, M. D. (1994). *Evaluation of the effects of programming arrangements on student learning outcomes* (NRC/GT Research Monograph). Charlottesville, VA: University of Virginia.

Elmore, R., & Zenus, V. (1994). Enhancing social-emotional development in middle school gifted students. *Roeper Review, 16,* 182–185.

Gamoran, A., Nystrand, M., & Berends, M. (1990, March). *Classroom instruction and the effects of ability grouping: A structured model.* Paper presented at the annual meeting of the American Educational Research Association, Boston.

Gentry, M. L. (1996, Spring). Total school cluster grouping: An investigation of achievement and identification of elementary school students. *NRC/GT Newsletter, 1–2,* 4.

Gentry, M. L. (1999). *Promoting student achievement and exemplary classroom practices through cluster grouping: A research-based alternative to heterogeneous elementary classrooms* (Research monograph for Office of Educational Research and Instruction.) Washington, DC: OERI. (ERIC Document Service Reproduction No. ED 429389)

Gross, M. U. M. (1997). Changing teacher attitudes to gifted students through inservice training. *Gifted and Talented International, 9,* 15–21.

Hafenstein, N. L., Jordan, N. E., & Tucker, B. (1993). *A descriptive study of multi-age grouping for primary gifted students.* Paper presented at the annual meeting of American Educational Research Association, Atlanta, GA. (ERIC Document Reproduction Service No. ED 360782)

Hernandez-Garduno, E. L. (1997). Effects of teaching problem solving through cooperative learning methods on student achievement, attitudes toward mathematics, mathematics self-efficacy, and metacognition. *NRC/GT Newsletter.* Storrs, CT: NRC/GT. (ERIC Document Reproduction Service No. ED 436908)

Hollingsworth, P. M., & Harrison, G. V. (1999). Comparing whole class with traditional grouping: First grade reading instruction. *Reading Improvement, 14,* 183–187.

Kanevsky, L. (1985). Computer-based math for gifted students: Comparison of cooperative and competitive strategies. *Journal for the Education for the Gifted, 8,* 239–255.

Keller, J. (1991*). Self-perception and the grouping of gifted children.* Paper presented at the annual meeting of the American Educational Research Association, Chicago. (ERIC Document Reproduction Service No. ED 334725)

Kennedy, D. M. (2002). Glimpses of a highly gifted child in a heterogeneous classroom. *Roeper Review, 24,* 120–125.

Kenny, D. A., Archambault, F. X., & Hallmark, B. W. (1995). *The effects of group composition on gifted and non-gifted elementary students in cooperative learning groups* (Research Monograph No. 95116.) Storrs, CT: NRC/GT. (ERIC Document Reproduction Service No. ED 402702)

Kulik, J. A. (1993). *An analysis of the research on ability grouping.* Paper developed for the Research-Based Decision Making Series. Storrs, CT: National Research Center on the Gifted and Talented.

Kulik, J. A., & Kulik, C-L. C. (1992). Meta-analytic findings on grouping programs. *Gifted Child Quarterly, 36,* 73–77.

Lim, T. K. (1994). Letters to themselves: Gifted students' plans for positive lifestyles. *Roeper Review, 17,* 85–80.

Lloyd, L. (1999). Multi-age classes and high ability students. *Review of Educational Research, 69,* 187–212.

Lou, Y., Abrami, P. C., Spence, J. C., Poulsen, C., Chambers, B., & d'Apollonia, S. (1996). Within-class grouping: A meta-analysis. *Review of Educational Research, 66,* 423–458.

Lynch, S. (1993). *The gifted and talented at Walbrook High: A restructured school in Baltimore, Maryland.* Paper presented at the annual meeting of American Education Research Association, Atlanta, GA. (ERIC Document Reproduction Service No. ED 360784)

Martin, J., Powers, L., Ward, J., & Webb, M. (2000). *Empowering intrinsic learners.* Master's degree research project, St. Xavier

University, Chicago. (ERIC Document Reproduction Service No. ED 445776)

Mousley, J. A. (1998). Ability grouping: Some implications for building mathematical understanding. *Teaching mathematics in new times: Proceedings of the annual conference of the Mathematics Education Research Group of Australasia. Vol. 2,* 32-47. (ERIC Document Reproduction Service No. ED 429813)

Neber, H., Finsterwald, M., & Urban, N. (2001). Cooperative learning with gifted and high achieving students: A review and meta-analysis of 12 studies. *High Ability Students, 12,* 199–214.

Rogers, K. (1991). *The relationship of grouping practices to the education of the gifted and talented learner: An executive summary.* Storrs, CT: The National Research Center on the Gifted and Talented.

Roy, A. (1990, November). *A meta-evaluation of Johnson and Johnson's meta-analysis of research on cooperative learning.* Paper presented at the annual meeting of the National Association for Gifted Children, Cincinnati, OH.

Schuler, P.A. (1997, Winter). Cluster grouping coast to coast. *NRC/GT Newsletter,* 1,4.

Shields, C. M. (2002). A comparison study of student attitudes and perceptions in homogeneous and heterogeneous classrooms. *Roeper Review, 24,* 115–120.

Sizer, T. R. (1984). *Horace's compromise: Study of high schools.* New York: Houghton Mifflin.

Sizer, T. R. (1992). *Horace's hope: What works for the American high school.* New York: Houghton Mifflin.

Sizer, T. R. (1996). *Horace's school: Redesigning the American high school.* New York: Houghton Mifflin.

Slavin, R. S. (1987). Ability grouping: A best-evidence synthesis. *Review of Educational Research, 57,* 293–336.

Stout, J. (1993). *The use of cooperative learning with elementary gifted students: Practical and theoretical implications.* Paper presented at the annual meeting of the American Educational Research Association, Atlanta, GA. (ERIC Document Reproduction Service No. ED 360783)

Vaughn, V. L., Feldhusen, J F., & Asher, J.W. (1991). Meta-analysis and review of research on pull-out programs in gifted education. *Gifted Child Quarterly, 35,* 92–98.

Zeidner, M., & Schleyer, E. J. (1999). The effects of educational context on individual difference variables, self-perceptions of giftedness, and school attitudes of gifted adolescents. *Journal of Youth and Adolescence, 28*, 687–705.

Karen B. Rogers is currently director of research for GER-RIC (Gifted Education Research and Resource Information Centre) and professor of education in the Faculty of Arts and Social Sciences at the University of New South Wales in Sydney, Australia. She is on a 3-year leave from the University of St. Thomas in Minneapolis, MN. In 1991 she wrote *The Relationship of Grouping Practices to the Education of Gifted and Talented Learners* for the National Research Center on the Gifted and Talented. This monograph represents an update of extant research since that report. She is coeditor of *Talent in Context: Historical and Social Perspectives* and author of *Re-forming Gifted Education: Matching the Program to the Child,* published in 2002. She has written more than 90 articles for scholarly journals and magazines, 14 chapters for books, and has conducted more than 60 evaluations of programs in which grouping has or has not been an option for gifted children. She is a past-president of The Association of the Gifted (TAG) and is on the editorial boards of *Gifted Child Quarterly, Roeper Review, Journal for the Education of the Gifted, Journal of Secondary Gifted Education,* and *Gifted and Talented International.*

Printed in the United States
by Baker & Taylor Publisher Services